The Whiz

by Mark Decker
illustrated by Len Epstein

Core Decodable 47

McGraw Hill Education

Bothell, WA • Chicago, IL • Columbus, OH • New York, NY

MHEonline.com

McGraw-Hill Education

Send all inquiries to:
McGraw-Hill Education
8787 Orion Place
Columbus, OH 43240

ISBN: 978-0-02-136221-9
MHID: 0-02-136221-1

Printed in Canada.

9 10 11 12 KOD 24

This is the Whiz.

When the Whiz starts, it chugs up and up.

When it is at the top, the Whiz stops.

Wham! The Whiz whips left.
Wham! The Whiz whips back.

The Whiz whips up a big hill.
Then it whips past a bridge.

Wham! When the Whiz stops, it stops fast.